take it apart

PLANE

By Chris Oxlade

Illustrated by George Fryer

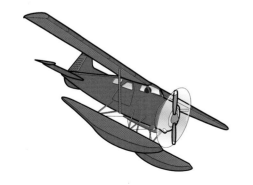
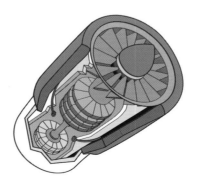
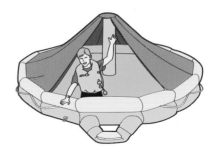

Thameside Press

US publication copyright © 2002 Thameside Press.
International copyright reserved in all countries.
No part of this book may be reproduced in any form
without written permission from the publisher.

Distributed in the United States by
Smart Apple Media
1980 Lookout Drive
North Mankato, MN 56003

Text copyright © Chris Oxlade
Illustrator copyright © George Fryer

ISBN 1-930643-95-0

Library of Congress Control Number 2002 141349

Editor: Jilly MacLeod
Designer: Guy Callaby
Illustrator: George Fryer
Consultants: Lindsay Peacock and Elizabeth Atkinson

Printed by South China Printing Co. Ltd., Hong Kong

Inside this Book

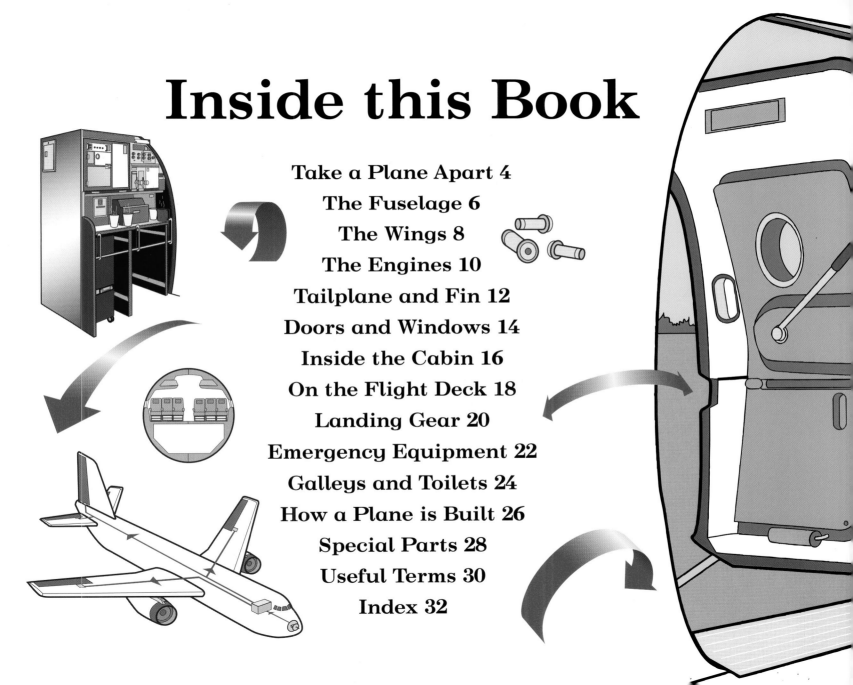

Take a Plane Apart

- A plane is made of tens of thousands of different parts.

- The parts are made of metal, plastic, rubber, glass, and many other special materials.

- All the parts are put together in an aircraft factory.

- This book shows you the main parts of an airliner (a large passenger plane) and how they fit together.

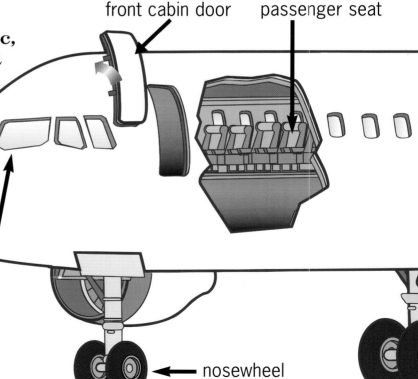

front cabin door

passenger seat

flight deck

nosewheel

4

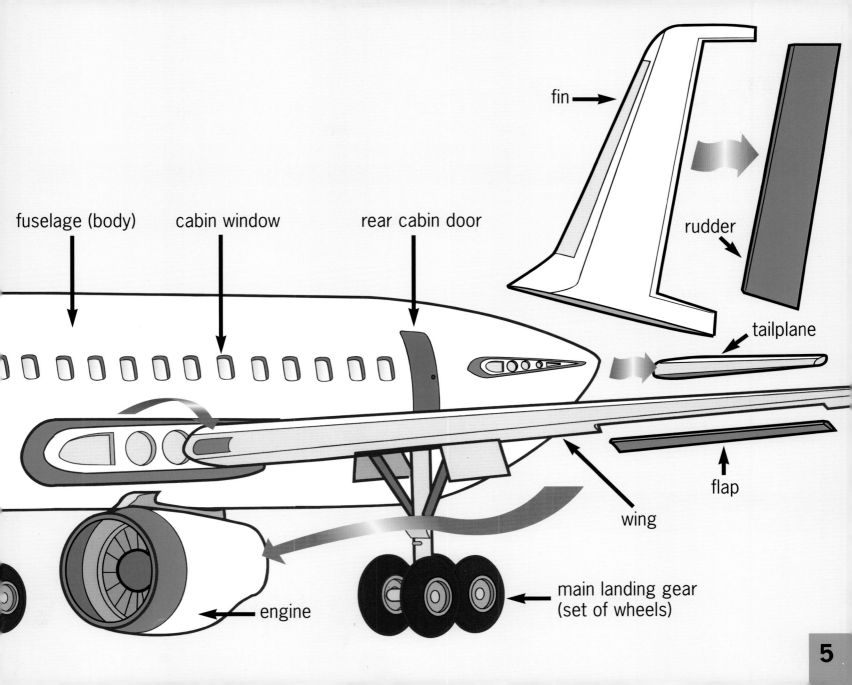

fin

rudder

fuselage (body)

cabin window

rear cabin door

tailplane

wing

flap

engine

main landing gear
(set of wheels)

The Fuselage

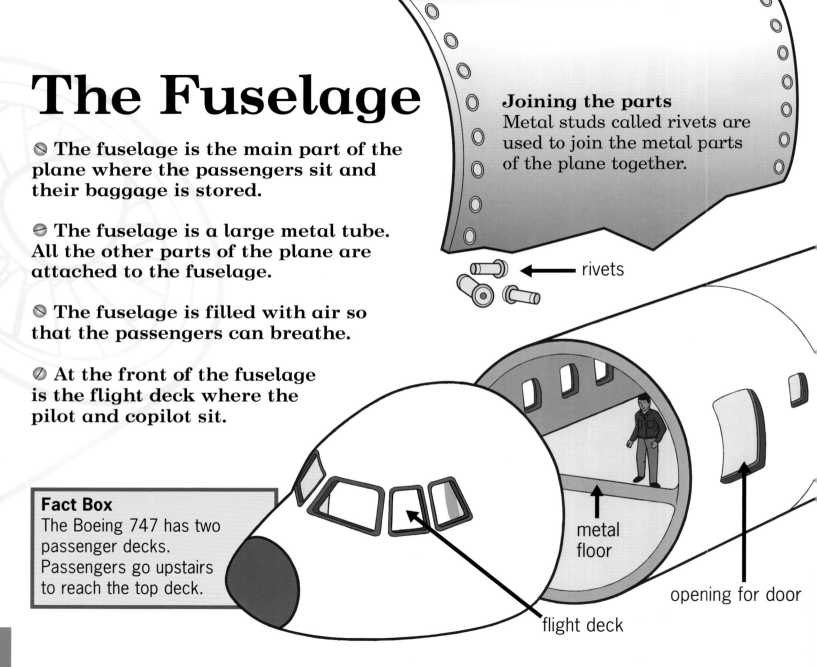

- The fuselage is the main part of the plane where the passengers sit and their baggage is stored.

- The fuselage is a large metal tube. All the other parts of the plane are attached to the fuselage.

- The fuselage is filled with air so that the passengers can breathe.

- At the front of the fuselage is the flight deck where the pilot and copilot sit.

Joining the parts
Metal studs called rivets are used to join the metal parts of the plane together.

rivets

Fact Box
The Boeing 747 has two passenger decks. Passengers go upstairs to reach the top deck.

metal floor

opening for door

flight deck

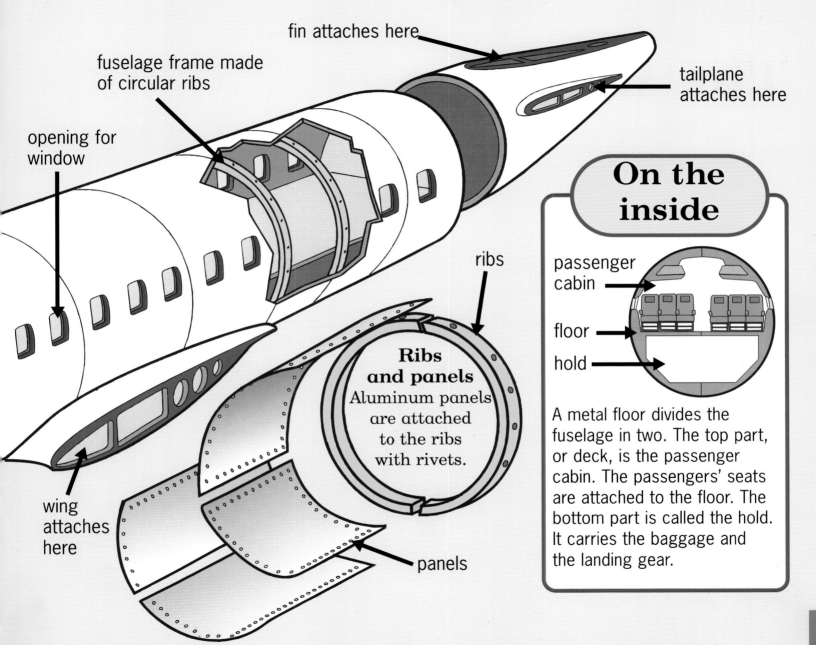

fin attaches here

fuselage frame made
of circular ribs

tailplane
attaches here

opening for
window

ribs

On the inside

passenger
cabin

floor

hold

**Ribs
and panels**
Aluminum panels
are attached
to the ribs
with rivets.

A metal floor divides the
fuselage in two. The top part,
or deck, is the passenger
cabin. The passengers' seats
are attached to the floor. The
bottom part is called the hold.
It carries the baggage and
the landing gear.

wing
attaches
here

panels

The Wings

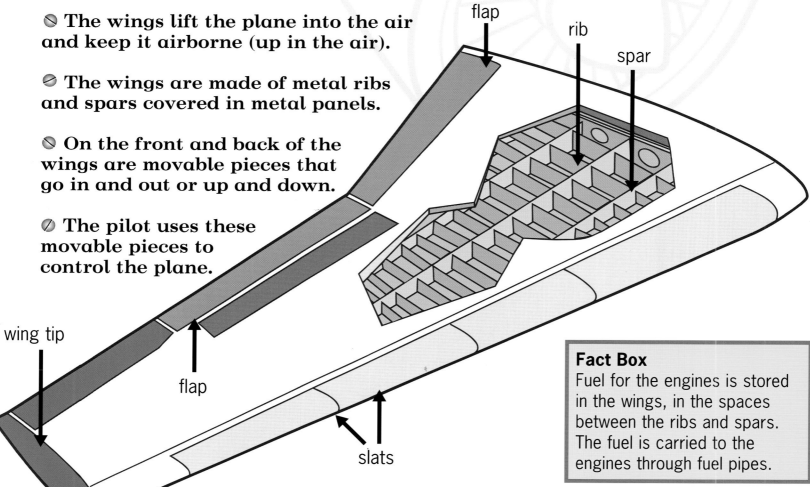

- The wings lift the plane into the air and keep it airborne (up in the air).

- The wings are made of metal ribs and spars covered in metal panels.

- On the front and back of the wings are movable pieces that go in and out or up and down.

- The pilot uses these movable pieces to control the plane.

flap

rib

spar

wing tip

flap

slats

Fact Box
Fuel for the engines is stored in the wings, in the spaces between the ribs and spars. The fuel is carried to the engines through fuel pipes.

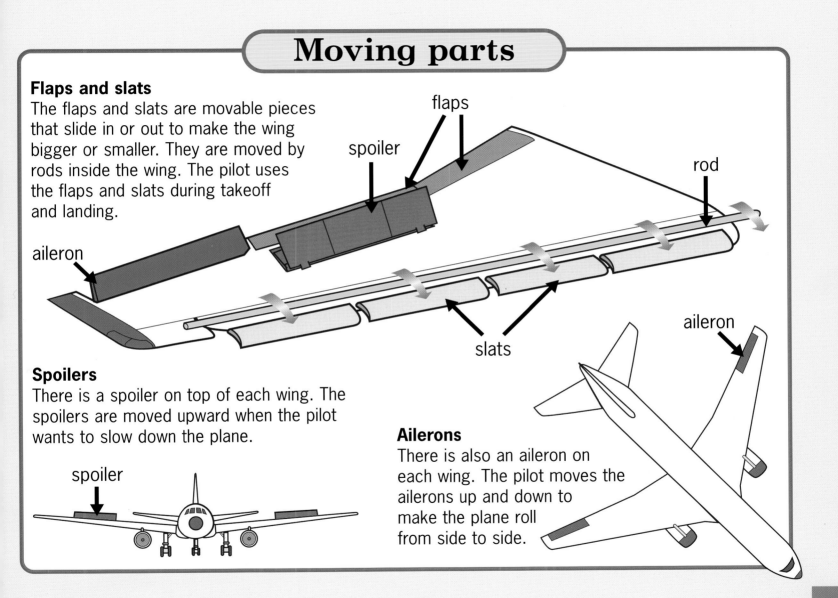

Moving parts

Flaps and slats
The flaps and slats are movable pieces that slide in or out to make the wing bigger or smaller. They are moved by rods inside the wing. The pilot uses the flaps and slats during takeoff and landing.

flaps

spoiler

rod

aileron

slats

aileron

Spoilers
There is a spoiler on top of each wing. The spoilers are moved upward when the pilot wants to slow down the plane.

spoiler

Ailerons
There is also an aileron on each wing. The pilot moves the ailerons up and down to make the plane roll from side to side.

The Engines

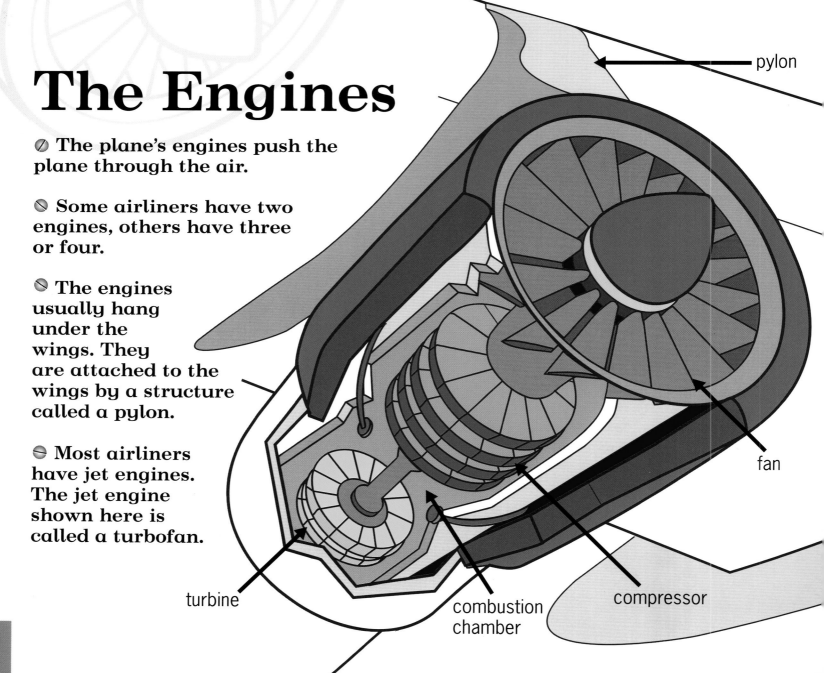

⊘ The plane's engines push the plane through the air.

◒ Some airliners have two engines, others have three or four.

◒ The engines usually hang under the wings. They are attached to the wings by a structure called a pylon.

◒ Most airliners have jet engines. The jet engine shown here is called a turbofan.

pylon

fan

turbine

combustion chamber

compressor

Ground power engine

There is also a small engine inside the tail. It works like the main engines but does not help the plane to fly. Instead, it makes electricity for the plane when it is on the ground.

ground power engine

How a jet engine works

1. Fan

A turbofan jet engine has a huge spinning fan at the front that sucks in air. Most of the air rushes straight through, but some air goes into the engine.

air in

2. Compressor

A spinning part inside the engine, called a compressor, squeezes the air into the combustion chamber.

4. Turbine

The hot gases rush backward out of the engine and drive the plane forward. The gases also turn the turbine, which makes the fan and the compressor spin around.

hot gases out

3. Combustion chamber

Inside the combustion chamber, the air is used to burn fuel. As the fuel burns, it makes a stream, or jet, of hot gases.

Tailplane and Fin

🔘 **The tailplane keeps the plane flying level.**

🔘 **The fin stops the plane swaying from side to side.**

🔘 **There is a movable piece on the fin called the rudder, and two on the tailplane called the elevators.**

🔘 **The pilot uses the rudder and elevators to steer the plane.**

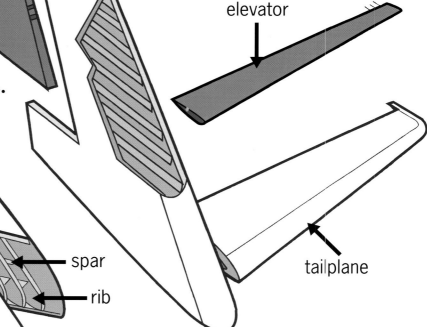

rudder

fin

elevator

tailplane

tailplane

spar

outer skin

rib

12

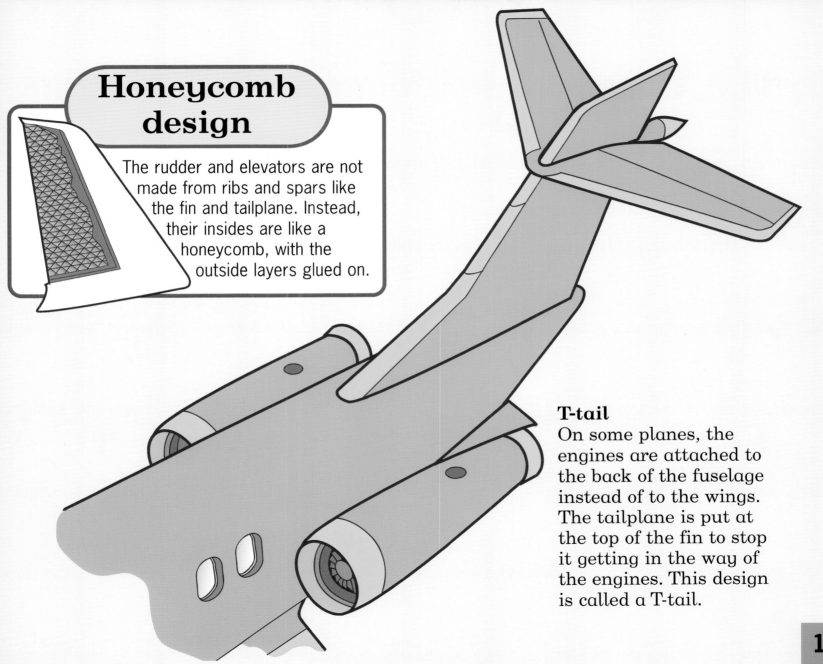

Honeycomb design

The rudder and elevators are not made from ribs and spars like the fin and tailplane. Instead, their insides are like a honeycomb, with the outside layers glued on.

T-tail
On some planes, the engines are attached to the back of the fuselage instead of to the wings. The tailplane is put at the top of the fin to stop it getting in the way of the engines. This design is called a T-tail.

Doors and Windows

- The passengers get on and off the plane through cabin doors in the side of the fuselage.

- The doors are tightly closed before the plane takes off.

- Huge doors under the plane open into the baggage hold.

- There are windows along both sides of the cabin and at the front of the flight deck.

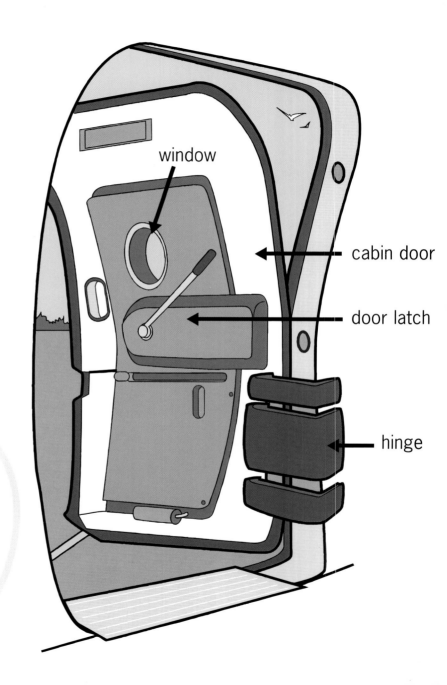

window

cabin door

door latch

hinge

Getting on and off

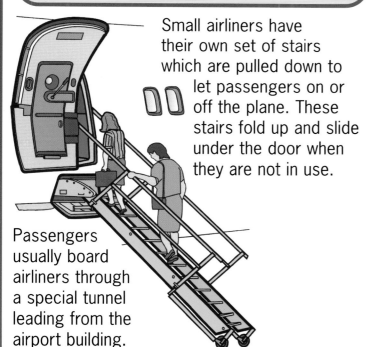

Small airliners have their own set of stairs which are pulled down to let passengers on or off the plane. These stairs fold up and slide under the door when they are not in use.

Passengers usually board airliners through a special tunnel leading from the airport building.

Fact Box
The flight deck windows even have windshield wipers, just like a car.

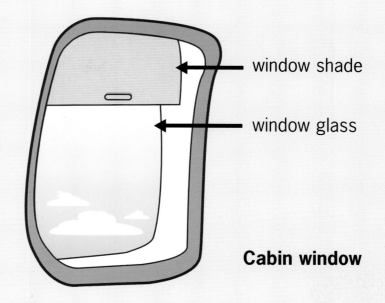

window shade

window glass

Cabin window

Flight deck windows
The windows in the flight deck give the pilot and copilot a good all-around view. They are much bigger than the passenger windows and have very thick glass.

Inside the Cabin

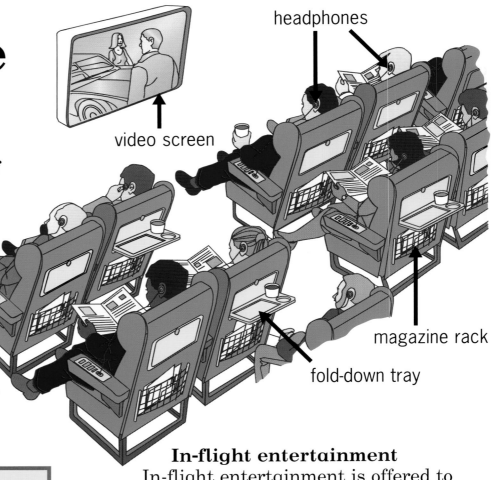

video screen

headphones

magazine rack

fold-down tray

◢ The cabin contains rows of seats for the passengers.

◢ Each seat has a seat belt for safety.

◢ In front of each passenger is a fold-down tray and a magazine rack.

◢ Above the passengers' heads are storage lockers for coats and bags.

Fact Box
The seats and other parts of the cabin are made of materials that do not burn easily. This helps to prevent fires from starting.

In-flight entertainment
In-flight entertainment is offered to passengers on long flights. They can use headphones to listen to music or watch movies on video screens.

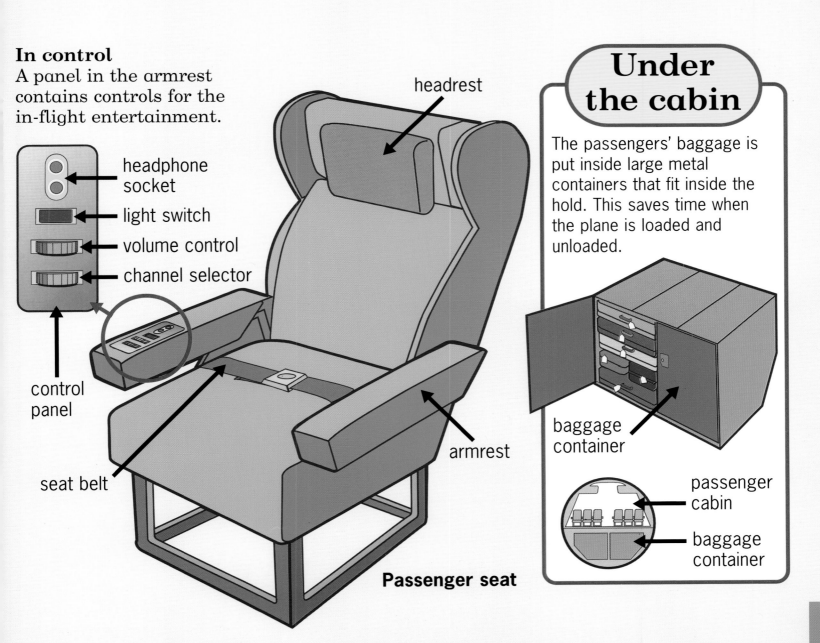

In control
A panel in the armrest contains controls for the in-flight entertainment.

headphone socket

light switch

volume control

channel selector

control panel

seat belt

headrest

armrest

Passenger seat

Under the cabin

The passengers' baggage is put inside large metal containers that fit inside the hold. This saves time when the plane is loaded and unloaded.

baggage container

passenger cabin

baggage container

On the Flight Deck

◉ The flight deck is where the pilot and copilot sit.

◉ It contains all the controls and switches that the pilots need to fly the plane.

◉ Instruments give the pilots information about the plane, such as how much fuel is left and how fast the plane is going.

◉ Many miles of electric wiring lead from the flight deck to all parts of the plane.

Radar screen

Weather detector
At the front of the plane is an electronic machine called a radar. It can detect bad weather ahead. The pilots view the radar pictures on a screen on the flight deck.

Fly-by-wire

In older airliners, pilots control the flaps, slats, and other movable parts directly, using a system of rods and levers. In some modern airliners, the movable parts are controlled by computers instead. This is called fly-by-wire.

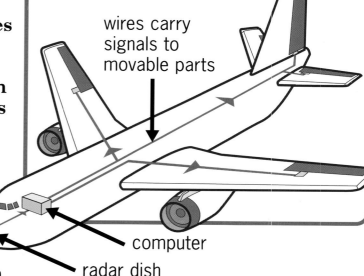

wires carry signals to movable parts

computer

radar dish

18

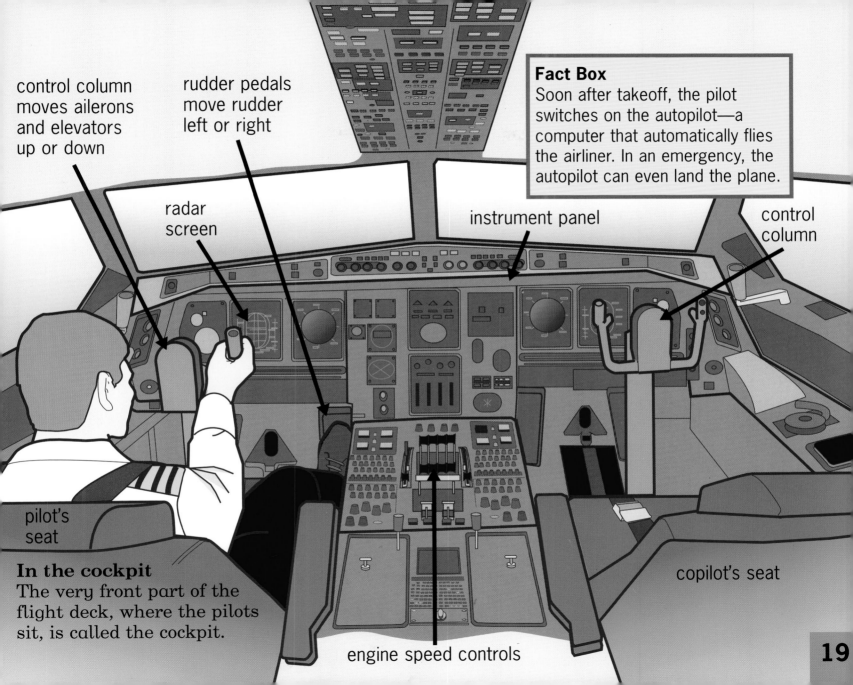

control column
moves ailerons
and elevators
up or down

rudder pedals
move rudder
left or right

Fact Box
Soon after takeoff, the pilot
switches on the autopilot—a
computer that automatically flies
the airliner. In an emergency, the
autopilot can even land the plane.

radar
screen

instrument panel

control
column

pilot's
seat

In the cockpit
The very front part of the
flight deck, where the pilots
sit, is called the cockpit.

copilot's seat

engine speed controls

Landing Gear

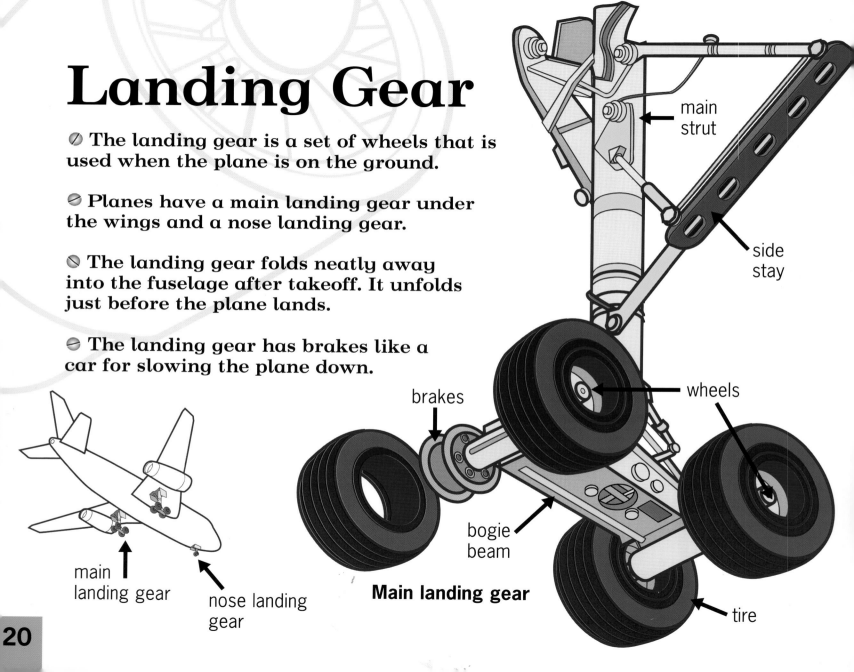

- The landing gear is a set of wheels that is used when the plane is on the ground.

- Planes have a main landing gear under the wings and a nose landing gear.

- The landing gear folds neatly away into the fuselage after takeoff. It unfolds just before the plane lands.

- The landing gear has brakes like a car for slowing the plane down.

main strut

side stay

brakes

wheels

bogie beam

main landing gear

nose landing gear

tire

Main landing gear

Landing Gear

After takeoff, the landing gear folds away into an opening in the fuselage and wing. Doors close over the opening to give the plane a smooth shape so that it cuts cleanly through the air.

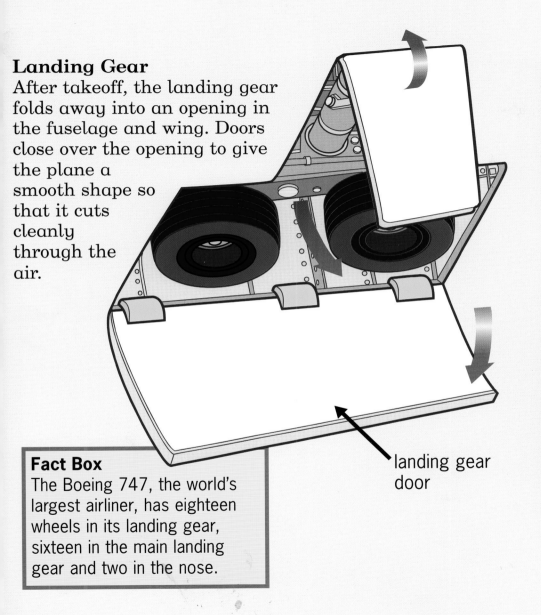

landing gear door

Fact Box
The Boeing 747, the world's largest airliner, has eighteen wheels in its landing gear, sixteen in the main landing gear and two in the nose.

Tires

An airliner lands at over 125 miles an hour. When the tires hit the runway, they get very hot. If they were filled with air the tires might explode, so they are filled with a special gas instead.

Emergency Equipment

An airliner has special equipment for helping the passengers and crew in an emergency.

Emergency exits from the cabin help people make a quick escape.

Every passenger and crew member has an inflatable (blow-up) life jacket in case the plane has to land in the sea.

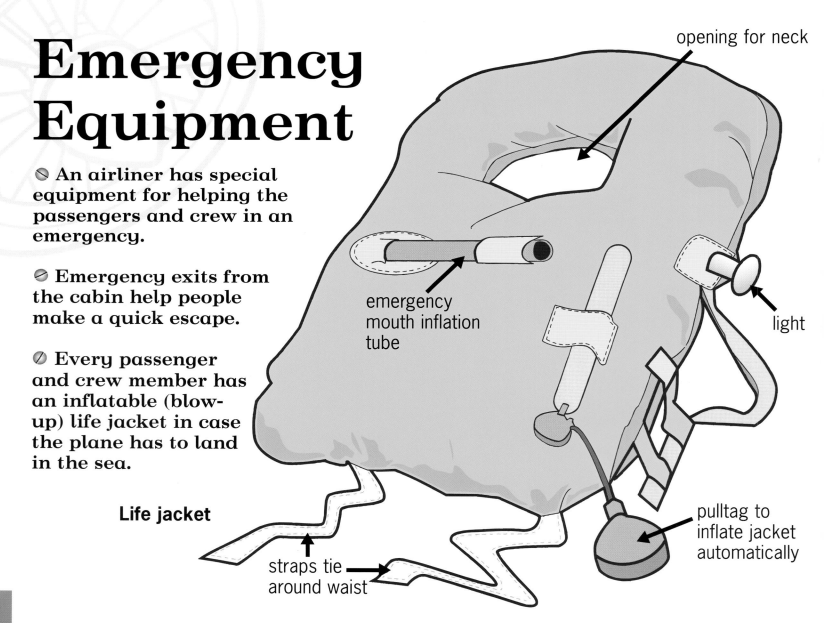

Life jacket

opening for neck

emergency mouth inflation tube

light

pulltag to inflate jacket automatically

straps tie around waist

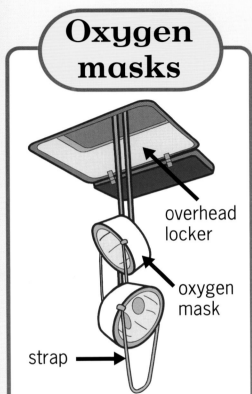

Oxygen masks

overhead locker

oxygen mask

strap

Oxygen masks are stored in the overhead lockers. They come down automatically if the air escapes from the cabin. Passengers strap the masks over their nose and mouth to breathe in oxygen.

Emergency slides

If passengers have to leave the cabin quickly, emergency slides are used. The slides are stored in a box inside the cabin doors.

emergency slide

Life rafts

Some planes carry inflatable life rafts, in case the plane has to land in the sea.

Fact Box
Aircraft engines have their own fire extinguishers. If an engine catches fire, the pilot operates the fire extinguishers from the flight deck.

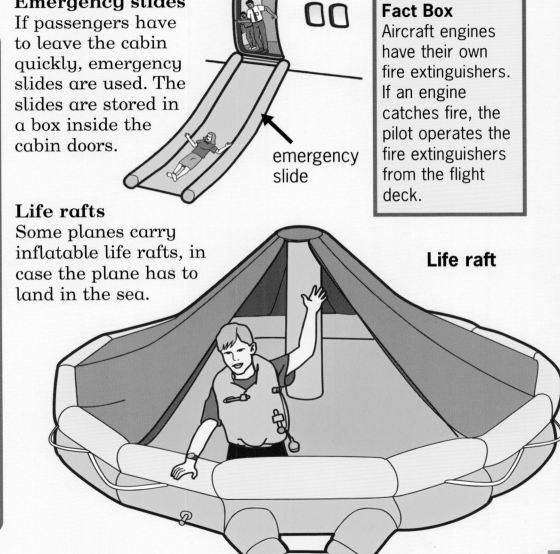

Life raft

Galleys and Toilets

- The galley is where the cabin staff prepare meals for the passengers.

- The galley has microwave ovens, pots, and places to store food and drinks.

- Hot meals are cooked before they are put on the plane. They are stored in heated containers in the galley.

- The bathrooms have toilets and sinks for the passengers.

Fact Box
On a Boeing 747 flight from New York to London, the cabin crew may serve over a thousand meals to the passengers.

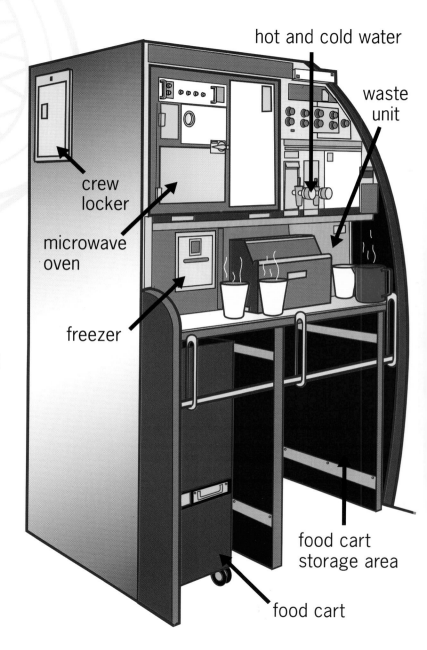

hot and cold water

waste unit

crew locker

microwave oven

freezer

food cart storage area

food cart

Feeding the passengers

Food and drinks are taken on food carts to the passengers. Each person is given a tray complete with food, utensils, napkin, cup and glass, and is offered a choice of drinks. When the food carts are not being used, they are locked into place in the galley.

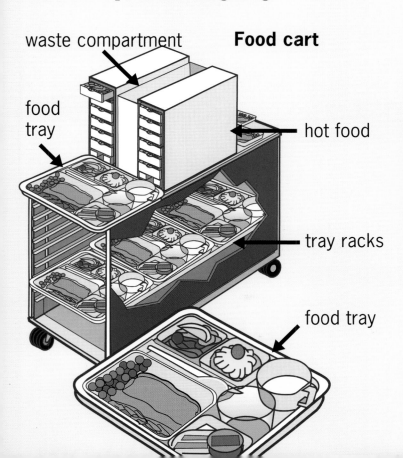

Food cart

waste compartment

food tray

hot food

tray racks

food tray

Getting rid of waste

Huge tanks in the hold store any waste from the toilets until the plane lands at an airport. Then the waste is sucked into a truck and taken away for disposal.

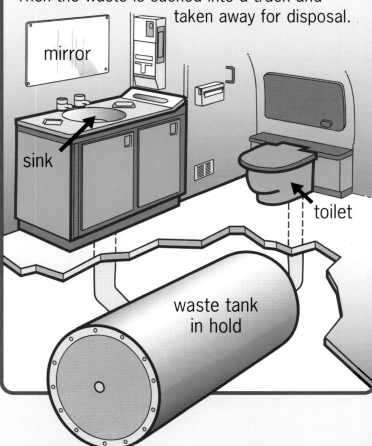

mirror

sink

toilet

waste tank in hold

How a Plane is Built

● Airliners are very large and have to be put together in enormous buildings.

◐ Different parts of the plane are made in different factories. Then they are taken to the main factory to be put together.

◑ It takes many months to build a plane.

The fuselage and wings
The fuselage is made from short sections joined together. The wings attach to the middle section. All the parts rest on special supports while they are being joined together

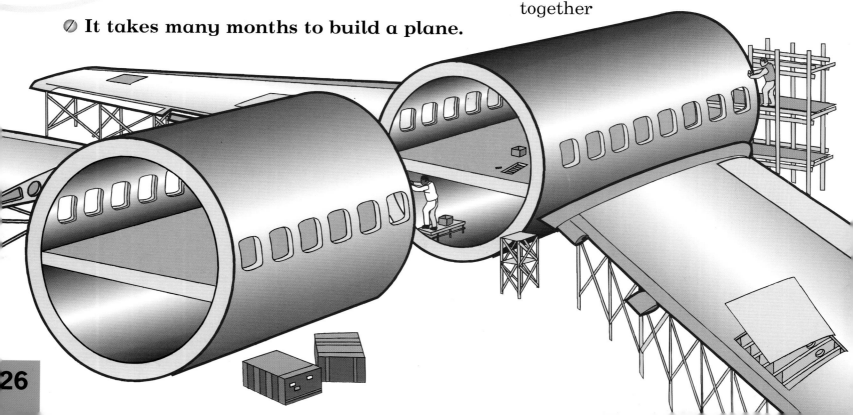

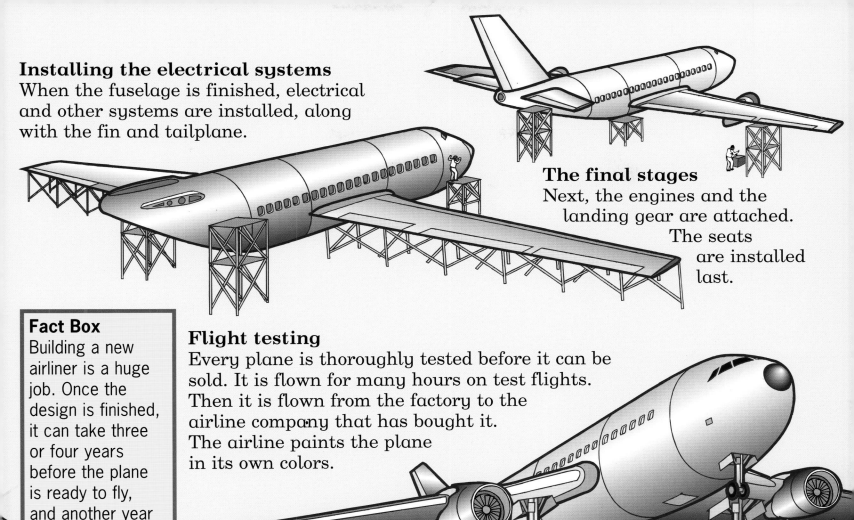

Installing the electrical systems

When the fuselage is finished, electrical and other systems are installed, along with the fin and tailplane.

The final stages

Next, the engines and the landing gear are attached. The seats are installed last.

Fact Box

Building a new airliner is a huge job. Once the design is finished, it can take three or four years before the plane is ready to fly, and another year or two before it is delivered to the airlines.

Flight testing

Every plane is thoroughly tested before it can be sold. It is flown for many hours on test flights. Then it is flown from the factory to the airline company that has bought it. The airline paints the plane in its own colors.

Special Parts

● Some planes do special jobs.

● They have different parts from other planes or extra parts that most planes do not have.

● You can see some of these special parts on this spread.

Floats
In countries where there are many lakes, such as Canada, planes have to be able to land on water. They have floats on their landing gear instead of wheels.

Propellers
Many planes have propellers on their engines to drive the plane forward. Propeller-powered planes are not as fast as jets, but they use less fuel and are cheaper to run.

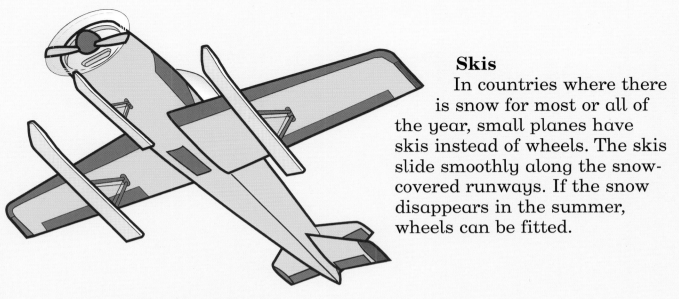

Skis

In countries where there is snow for most or all of the year, small planes have skis instead of wheels. The skis slide smoothly along the snow-covered runways. If the snow disappears in the summer, wheels can be fitted.

Front-opening cargo doors

Some planes have huge doors at the front, leading into the cargo (goods) hold. The doors allow big items, such as tanks or helicopters, to be loaded onto the plane.

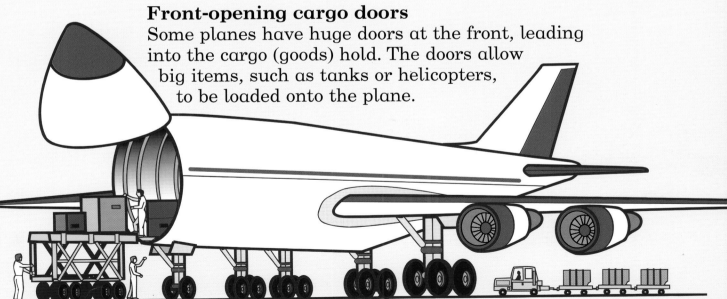

Useful Terms

aileron A panel toward the end of a plane's wing that is moved up or down to make the plane roll from side to side.

autopilot A computer that flies the plane automatically without the pilot's help.

baggage hold A space in the fuselage where the passengers' suitcases and bags are stored during a flight. It is normally under the cabin floor.

cockpit The front part of a plane's flight deck. It is where the pilot and copilot sit, surrounded by controls and instruments.

control column The control that the pilot holds when he or she is flying a plane. It moves the elevators and ailerons.

elevator A part on the back edge of the tailplane that is moved up and down to make the plane climb or descend.

fin The upright piece at the back of the fuselage. It helps to keep the plane flying straight.

flap A movable part on the back edge of the wing that slides out to make the wing bigger. The flaps are used during takeoff and landing.

flight deck The room at the front of a plane where the pilots sit and where all the plane's controls and instruments are.

fuselage The main part of a plane, where passengers sit and cargo is carried. All the other parts are attached to the fuselage.

galley A small kitchen in an airliner's cabin. Cabin staff prepare food and drinks in the galley.

ground power engine A small jet engine that makes electricity for the plane while the main engines are turned off.

jet engine A type of plane engine that sends a stream, (jet) of hot gases backward at very high speed, pushing the plane forward.

landing gear Sets of wheels under the plane that roll along while the plane is on the ground. On large planes, the landing gear folds away when the plane is flying. Smaller planes have a fixed landing gear, which does not fold away.

life raft An inflatable (blow-up) boat used in case a plane has to make an emergency landing at sea.

propeller engine An engine that makes a propeller (a set of long blades) spin around. This pushes the plane forward.

pylon The part of a plane that connects the plane's engines to its wings.

radar An electronic machine that is used to detect other planes nearby and bad weather.

rib A hoop of metal in a plane's fuselage. Rows of ribs make up the frame of the fuselage. Metal panels are attached to the ribs to form an outer shell.

rivet A metal fastener used for joining two pieces of metal together.

rudder A part on the back of a fin that is turned from side to side to make the plane turn from side to side.

slat A part on the front edge of the wing that slides out to make the wing bigger during takeoff and landing.

spar Part of a wing's frame that stretches from one end of the wing to the other. Spars stop the wing from bending too much.

spoiler A part on the back of the wing that lifts up to slow the plane down before it lands.

tailplane The small pair of wings at the back of the fuselage. The tailplane helps the plane to fly level.

turbofan A type of jet engine that is often used on large planes. It has a large fan in front of the engine to suck in air.

Index